"J.T. Knoll's book *Counterpart* is a breath of fresh cut grass and peaceful like a summer night. He leaves us wanting to know more about the small-town pool hall owner who watches over the high school kids and the neighbor lady who shares her peonies. He finds mercy in the elderly mother who has grown kinder as her memory grows softer. Like William Stafford and Carl Sandburg, Knoll writes clear and subtly insightful poems that draw on precise descriptions of the natural world. The big Kansas sky, the beloved dog, and the train run throughout the book. Knoll loves Kansas like one might love 'Cheerios and dandelion bracelets.' Anyone viewing Kansas through his eyes will love it, too."

—Beth Gruver Gulley, *The Sticky Note Alphabet*

"The poems in J.T. Knoll's excellent collection *Counterpart* manage to pull off the minor miracle of being both Kodachrome-saturated snapshots of memory and timeless. Shifting between a blue collar Kansas that may no longer exist and the present, Knoll creates a personal mythology of experience. This is poetry on a very human level, delivered at a time when we might desperately need it the most."

—Troy Schoultz, author of *No Quiet Entrances* and co-author of *Remnants*

"J.T. Knoll's poems consistently find the remarkable within the mundane; the spiritual, if not religious, within the secular. Some poems are lyrical, both humorous and ironic, songs to the living; others are hardscrabble from the coal mines, the railroad, the corner black market fireworks stand, alive with people, those we've known and possibly forgotten. *Counterpart* connects the ordinary to the extraordinary. Each poem is a tribute to our everyday communion with the transcendental. It's a book for the nightstand and for tomorrow."

— Al Ortolani, *Swimming Shelter*

"With precise, evocative language J.T. Knoll captures the essence of life in rural Kansas. Whether his subjects are coal miners, farmers, neighboring housewives or his own childhood, Knoll's poetry reminds us that by looking at the everyday world around us, by listening to human stories and by connecting to nature, we can find the spiritual in the quotidian. He makes the ordinary extraordinary."

— Elizabeth Winthrop Alsop, *Daughter of Spies: Wartime Secrets, Family Lies*

Counterpart

Poems by J.T. Knoll

Spartan Press

Kansas City   Missouri

Spartan Press

Kansas City, Missouri

spartanpress.com

Spartan
Press

Cover art: "Solitude" — Katharine Stelle Spigarelli

Author photo: Linda O'Nelio Knoll

Acknowledgments:

Some of these poems and songs were previously published in the following publications: *Poets to Come, Chiron Review, Coal City Review, Front Porch Review, 150 Kansas Poems, The Shining Years, Konza Project, Heartland, Bards Against Hunger* and *Poetrybay.*

Thank you to Jason Ryberg for giving this book a home as well as sharing his expertise in editing, layout, and design.

TABLE OF CONTENTS

For my little bride, Linda,
and Arlo the Labradorian.

If you know them,
your lives are better for it.

Everyone carries a shadow, and the less it is embodied in the individual's conscious life, the blacker and denser it is. At all counts, it forms an unconscious snag, thwarting our most well-meant intentions.

— Carl Jung

Counterpart

Some time in the twilight
ask me about my other
— whether or not what he has done is my life.
He has come and gone at will
and sometimes tried to help … or hurt.
Ask me what difference
his kindness or cruelty has made.
Then you and I can sit
and hold the hush between us.

Prepare For The Inevitable

I went to a small-town high school. To the basketball games Tuesday and Friday nights to watch a certain cheerleader and prepare for the inevitable. Bobby Dick would make all state, drop out of MU to wed Mary Snow, become an engineer on the Kansas City Southern Railroad and, years later, divorce and be seen at the Idle Hour, looking over at the cheerleader and me with a crooked smile of friendship. I would write a poem about the cheerleader's unapologetic way of being herself — a beauty who doesn't accept awards for it. After college, I followed her to Chicago where we set off on a life of joy, babies and hardship — returning, eventually, to the curious place that was home; she teaching gifted, me singing in the choir. Both of us the same even though we had become someone else.

On The Way Back

I look up from reading a mystery novel
to see impressionist brushstrokes —
Ethel working in her yard
across Euclid Street in an old straw hat.
Later that day, she walks over
and flags me down while I'm cutting grass
to tell me the peonies are in bloom;
that I'm welcome to come get all I want.
I grab a worn paring knife, cross the street
and walk up the red brick sidewalk to her yard.
She comes through the screen door,
eases her way down the worn steps
to visit as I carefully snip enough
pink peonies for a large bouquet.
On the way back home,
their scent pierces my memory
like a spear of fresh cut grass.

Cobb O'Hara

I'm a Democrat, a Catholic and a strong union man. In 1960 I quit pipe fittin' and opened a pool hall, O'Hara's Recreation. Bought Joe Doti's bar in Frontenac and set up two standards, a snooker and a one-pocket table. Also put in a grill for burgers. Served 'em up on a foot-square piece of waxed tissue, *Get 'em while they're hot, boys. They're good as mother's and better than others!* My wife, Erma, helped me out, which gave my place kind of a small town diner atmosphere. After a couple of years, I moved across the street to the site of the old Club Royale. Had a large adjoining room that I rented out for dances and a small back room where I'd take my cut out of the Saturday poker game. My place was the jumping off point for lots of the local boys, whether it was to the drive-in, a dance, a movie, or a ball game. Many ended their nights there, too — playing pinball as I brushed down and covered the silent tables, shut off the grill, and gave the last call. Sometimes I got a little brassy, but hell, I was running a pool hall. Kept an eye on the high school kids, though. Didn't let 'em drink underage in my place... but gave 'em a free 10 cent draft when they turned 18. Hell, Wilma Lavery said I was the cheapest babysitter she ever had.

Death Of A Farmer

Farmers,
foreheads blazing,
graceful in earth spirit,
gaze down at his mother
to see the fields they've worked
all their lives.

Deaf brother
wanders his white frame house,
points to his picture,
hears him signing
in the wind.

Twilight.
Wife wishes
she could be alone
with her children,
touching his breath
as fireflies dart
over green wheat.

Outside,
men in a circle drinking beer.
Best friend winks sorrowfully as I pass,
all the thoughts they never shared
tears on evening grass.

Easter Photo 1961

When I was a boy,
when Easter was still something special,
my older brothers took the window seats
while my sisters and I hung forward,
feet on the hump down the center of the floor,
Dad behind the wheel, Mother holding the baby,
everything simple,
ordinary as the catalpa trees
flickering past.

For all I knew every family was like ours,
aiming to the right along the highway's spine
to gather at Grandma's house by the evergreen,
a dog barking somewhere in the distance,
a passing scent on the wind,
a shutter's click.

Frank Bozick

I didn't want to go to school with five sisters, so I talked my mother into letting me work as a half-turn with Tom Kabonic in a little independent coal mine. Worked four days and stopped. It was killing my mother. So I became a mechanic. Drafted when I was 38 (everybody called me Pop), I landed at Omaha Beach five days after the Normandy Invasion. When we liberated Paris, my buddies and I got a Jeep, slipped in and spent a whole night there. Met a couple who took us to all the dance halls. Oh God! If it weren't for that, I woulda hated the Army! I liked to dance ... at least long enough to pick up a girl. I must've not picked up the right one, though ... been a bachelor all my life. It's like goin' to the store to buy a new pair of shoes, you know. Kinda hard to pick one pair out. Being a bachelor is a good life sometimes. ... sometimes it's not too good.

Grandpa Matt

grew up holding tools
— pounding, picking,
drilling and shoveling
rock face and coal
alongside his father
in the deep shafts,
which he entered at 12.
Above ground
he dug water lines,
sewer lines, gas lines,
foundations, and graves.
Weekends and evenings
he shoveled and raked
out back of his house,
mixing earth
with horse manure
to grow tomatoes,
beans, and potatoes.
I once asked him,
when he was
spading the garden,
how he did it,
day after day,
shovel after shovel
of rock, coal,
clay and dirt
all those years
in the mines.

He stopped and
gave me a quizzical look,
as if to say,
I'm not sure what you mean,
then kept on digging.

town talk bread

at second and broadway
ghost wall
i fall
into
toast and jelly
boy belly
paper route
inside out

miracle whip
and baloney
roy rogers
lunch box
ceremony

late night tv
black and white
movie ghosted
grandma's
peanut butter
sandwich smile
lightly-toasted

i ate some wild blackberries

still warm
from the sun
in memory of
dad
beside me
in the tangle
caressing each
berry like
an old love
mom
rolling dough
in a
snag of
light
on the
round oak
table
brother
eating cobbler
on the
back step
night birds
circling
slowly
overhead

I'm So Sorry

The spring after I got a Daisy Pump
for Christmas, I started picking off blue-green
insulators high on the electric wires
and plugging green apples on the tree
that grew up against our white frame garage.
Sometimes I practiced by placing a wooden
kitchen match ten feet or so away from the back steps
and trying to light it with a finely placed BB.

My first kill was a big blue jay that
was harassing my dog, King.
I picked off another jay
over on the neighbor's clothesline.
But when I shot a dove sitting alone
on the telephone line to the house,
I felt a great sadness.
So I went back to target shooting,
blasting dents in coffee cans,
shattering old pickle jars,
shooting spider webs into
the windows of the sagging, empty
house down by the Santa Fe tracks.

One day a young rabbit
hopped out from behind
our rusting trash barrel
and gazed at me innocently.

My gun came up involuntarily
and I shot him right in his unblinking eye.
He bolted straight up,
came down spinning and
whimpering in the grass.
I dropped my gun, broke into tears and
ran to kneel over him saying,
I'm sorry. I'm so sorry.

in kansas

- for father raphael, assumption abbey

we eat
chicken eggs
both white and brown
fry 'em for breakfast
and chow 'em down

for lunch, homegrown tomatoes
so round and so red
with bacon and lettuce
and hard crust bread

and fresh dug potatoes
so ruddy and small
boiled for supper
skins and all

in kansas

Jack Stanley

It all started when my dad gave me an old bicycle frame. I delivered groceries for Caspari's for 35 cents a day to buy parts. First I bought two wheels and a chain-and-sprocket, then one pedal, next a seat and then a basket ... and finally the other pedal. Then I got a paper route and saved enough to buy a brand-new Schwinn to which I attached a Whizzer motor. I rode that motorized bike to Joplin, Baxter Springs, and all points in between. Then it was on to Harleys. And then cars. When my car broke down and I couldn't afford to get it fixed, I did it myself. By sixteen I was maintaining diesel engines at Pittsburg's ice plant. You're born with it, the ability to take something apart and put it back together. A lot of it is just common sense. And you get common sense from having to survive.

Margaret

I had a lifetime penchant for clipping and saving whatever suited my fancy from the newspaper, starting at 15 with my grandmother's obituary notice. Lately, Tyson biting off a piece of Holyfield's ear, Clinton's Whitewater troubles, a beauty shop expanding to a full-service salon, Frontenac High School football games, lots of local wedding and anniversary announcements and, of course, obituaries. While I was living up in Kansas City, I collected song lyrics by jotting them down on scraps of paper at work, then transcribing them longhand into books — 15 all told. You might remember I mixed sodas and malts with Gertie behind the marble counter at Fedell's Drug Store in the 1950s. For five years before Fedell's, I took care of my bedridden mother. Once I forgot some anniversary or birthday and told her I was sorry — that I should have bought her some flowers. *You don't need to buy me no flowers, Margaret,* she said. *You're my flower.*

Strip Pit Enlightenment

While Buddha was awakened
Below a Bodhi tree
I woke beside a strip pit
That we all called Blue Sea

A cloud was passing over
Releasing whispers of cool rain
In tiny, tiny droplets
All different, all the same

Each made a little circle
Though they were but specs
Becoming one another
Each entering the next

The same is true of everything
Especially you and me
We are interwoven circles
Of love's geometry

That's It

My dad jitterbugged counterclockwise
on the hardwood to big bands
from his teens until
his back gave out in his mid-70s.

Danced with Mom in the kitchen
as *Rock Around the Clock* blared
on a dinky little 45 player.

Loved to sing, too.
We'd harmonize in the old Buick,
south on Highway 71, the 120 miles back home
from Chiefs games at old Municipal Stadium.

An engineer on the Kansas City Southern Railroad,
he'd sometimes croon *For the Good Times* or *Paper Doll*
on an open radio channel from K.C. to Shreveport.

In the early 1960s he bought an RCA console stereo
and hired Frank, the local TV repairman,
to wire it to the speaker of our upright television
to get an even more pronounced "split."

One day, not long afterward, when he was listening
to Sil Austin play *Danny Boy* on tenor sax,
I walked into the living room
to find him sitting in a chair positioned
halfway between both speakers.

He waved me over to his side.
Listen, he said,
his eyes welling with tears.
That's it.

That's Three Cents!

I was a Frontenac, Kansas bootlegger
every 4th of July back in the mid 1960s.
Cherry Bombs, Bulldogs, and M-80s hidden
under the 1 x 12 pine counter that displayed
Black Cats, parachutes, bottle rockets,
Lady Fingers, snakes, sparklers,
and assorted nightworks.
All surrounded by 2 x 4s and chicken wire
with a tin roof. Built it myself.
Great location — at the intersection where
Highway 160 turns north on its way
to the Missouri state line — directly across
from Sam Cicero's filling station, and its small town scenes
played out between clangs of the pneumatic black hose.
Locals sat in their cars like sultans as Sam hurried out
from the hoist where he was changing oil,
wiping his hands on a red shop rag, saying,
Filler up, Jay? She's high-test ... aaand antiknock
... aaand tailor-made by Senator Kerr and Mr. McGee.
The famous Kerr-McGee of Oklahoma.
Then, as he popped the hood, *Check your water,*
oil, aaand battery water at the same time?
This was followed by spirited Q and A
about work, family, ballgames, etc.
as he circled from pump to hood and back.
Around two in the afternoon it would get to be about
110 degrees under the tin roof, so I'd grab a dime
out of the cigar box I used to make change,
walk over to Sam's, pull a NuGrape from the jaws

of the horizontal Pepsi cooler, and head back,
as Sam called over my shoulder,
Aaand don't forget to bring back the bottle, Jay.
That's three cents!

The neighbors

beat the summer heat
with one of those old
swamp coolers that blew air
over water that fed to it through
a rubber garden hose connected to the hydrant.
We had a giant window fan that
pulled the curtains horizontal,
but it wasn't much good until 10 o' clock at night.
They were also the first on the block
to get a color TV, a Sylvania.
I didn't especially like going over there
(something about the way their
house smelled), but in late Kansas summer
I knew enough to accept an invitation
to watch the Yankees
play the White Sox on the
Saturday Game of the Week.
And so, I went crunching over
our adjoining gravel driveways
to their drawn drapes,
their cool, damp air,
their old brown couch,
their flickering colors.

The two years I sang in a soul band

I split the smoky air
all over Southeast Kansas.
Could smell a new perfume
in the dance halls and teen towns.
Came to understand that I'd been living
too long without making music.
My brand-new life had a spirit
that both worried and excited me.

I'd sometimes become James Brown on my knees,
the band hot behind me, sax blowing through me,
the dancers' bodies taut as they stopped to watch,
musky necklaces of sex and sweat glowing.
All sins forgiven by the music.

When my voice gave out, the band broke up.
I sold my microphone and moved on,
worry and excitement flickering along beside me
as I angled off toward the world I live in now.

Hod Carrier

Summers in college I worked as a hod carrier for Oheme Brothers Masonry, hauling brick and block, building scaffold and shoveling mortar. Roagie, the laborer foreman, knew my dad, chain-smoked Chesterfields, called me "Lefty's kid." One blistering June afternoon, when I'd sweated my jeans and t-shirt soggy, I asked him if he had any salt tablets. "HAW!" he exclaimed in a glee so loud all the bricklayers on the scaffold turned in unison. "SALT TABLETS? WHY NO, I DON'T THINK SO, SON!! SAY, DO ANY OF YOU BRICKLAYERS UP THERE HAVE ANY *SALT TABLETS* FOR THIS LABORER? HE'S FEELING A LITTLE POORLY!" This set off a flurry of activity on the line as Muse, Rocky, Joe, Claude, and Dog Man mumbled about salt tablets as they rummaged through their tool bags. One by one they called back, "Sorry, I took my last one," "Nope, none here," "Can't find mine," "I'll bring you some tomorrow." All summer I worked alongside the men, smiling at whatever good-natured salt tablet razz came my way. Returning to school in September, I found the classrooms hollow, some days driving to their work site after my last class to park a little ways off and watch, not wanting to lose touch with the part of me that was one of them.

I Say It's The Moon

Which is louder at a.m. 4:30
when walking with a black Lab
the back streets of a small Kansas town:

A hot-shot freight angling in from the south,
its horn tromboning longs and shorts,
sounding the aching steel on steel
of freight cars, oil tankers, flat cars, coal cars
(but no caboose ... never anymore a caboose)
all overlaid by the diesel electric OOOMMM
of a thousand Buddhist monks?

Or is it the moon?
The full, perfect purity of July moon,
following from the starlit, navy blue west,
calling its ancient mooncall of silence?

I say it's the moon.

The Kind Of Love I Have

I love you, Kansas.

I love you with the kind of love
I've had for Cheerios
since I was six.

For old catalpa trees,
fenderless bikes,
and the prize nestled
deep in the Cracker Jack box.

For the branch hanging low
over the farm pond,
the slanted light on corn field stubble,
and the rusted, red tractor working
its way down the mile section road.

For kitchen curtains,
Grandma's sewing machine
and dandelion bracelets.

For long walks home
on summer nights with my dog,
the tinsel of starlight
propping my heart open
for something large.

First Light

An inbound freight sounds
from the tracks east of town.
A woman smokes on her porch.
A man walks down the street saying the rosary.
A boy leans over the table eating cereal.

A dog yawns and stretches,
shuffles across the grass
to test his chain.

Late October

Cold enough here in Pittsburg, Kansas to wear a sweatshirt under my hoodie, which is to say I'm more like Arlo, who always wears two layers of Labradorian and now is grateful to have them; like the homeless man under the Lutheran church portico wrapped in a sleeping bag and blue tarp. I folded a 20 into Stafford's smoke signal poem and gave it to him last Wednesday in a cold drizzle that kept telling me, *Just go. Go on home and climb back in bed because life is miserable and the burdens of it show no sign of letting up.* But after the homeless man said, *Thank you, have a good day,* I kept on — not quite sure why but knowing why wouldn't have made any difference. Anyway, I had a sweatshirt under my hoodie.

november

blackbirds carve cold air
in tai chi grace above me
winter is coming

neighbor's patio
a metal chair meditates
like old trappist monk

pop, pop, of nail gun
neighbor shingles roof alone
not much daylight left

winter sycamore
bathed in the afternoon light
a sculpture in bone

nightfall in driveway
basketball hoop disappears
time to eat supper

January 5, 2021, 5 a.m.

As I circle Lakeside Park an outbound Kansas City Southern freight train trombones loud, and I mean LOUD, a horn song that enters and passes through me as it echoes through town. Echoes? Yes, echoes. How does it do that? I'm in Southeast Kansas. We have no canyons, no arroyos, no valleys. But it does. And then, boy-oh-boy, it sounds and echoes again … and again … as the diesel engine ooommms and growls, dragging its cargo through town and on south to Joplin, Sallisaw, Shreveport and Port Arthur. *This is my morning monk call to Lauds*, I think to myself. So I chant — in call and response with the horn — *O God, come to my assistance. O Lord, make haste to help me.* Our prayer pulsates and swells to a crescendo … then slowly descends and fades to silence as the train gathers speed and rolls on out of earshot. In its place, the drone of a single engine plane somewhere up above.

our tracks a helix

morning freezing rain
spruce trees bending low in yard
whom do they bow to?

winter wind blowing
across kansas plains aching
for branch to caress

locomotive om
sounds through heavy winter fog
morning diesel chant

winter's first snowfall
walking with my labrador
our tracks a helix

sunday

old pickup idling
om, om, om, om, om, om, om,
my meditation

three white puffs of cloud
low angling north, fast and pure
oh baby, baby

at sunday service
young preacher / old testament
no room for jesus

deep in the ozarks
monks silent in the abbey
their mojo working

afternoon snowfall
in st. mary's parking lot
young priest does doughnuts

nothing comes to mind

6 a.m. again
wondering what day it is
i pull on gray socks

kcs freight train
diesel omm and trombone horn
take up last night's slack

red fox glances up
wistful and lonely for love
below the street sign

listening for poems
ahead of me / behind me
words staggering in

january sixth
feast of the epiphany
nothing comes to mind

Saturday Night At The V.F.W.

- for James Tate

as the toothless, fat girl
in the MIDNIGHT ANGEL sweatshirt
was dancing with the
barefoot albino,
Taxi flashed me a metallic smile
and asked if I ever wondered
what it would be like
to be brain dead.

Later,
I heard the midnight angel
say to the albino,
"Electrocute me with your prod, baby.
I wanna light up like neon."

Outside,
a dense fog was coming in.

Slade

Every day for twenty years
I watched them carry Slade
to the chopper in a bag.
Sometimes as I shaved;
others when I sat at my desk at work,
or made love to my wife.

And no one knew but me
and the vodka
and the coke.

He begged me that day
to change his assignment.
If only ...

Christ, Slade, I had no way to know.

You know,
I never even had a real fight
before I went to Vietnam.

And it's not just Slade, man.
It's the killing.
I always felt worse
about setting an ambush
than getting hit by one.

Another thing,
men don't die like they show
in the movies and on TV.
They scream
and call for their mommas.

A Couple Of Good Reminders

There's nothing quite like the odor of a good shit
the morning after devouring a couple of
big baskets of freshly-cut, battered
and deep-fried onion rings
out at the Idle Hour.
The odor drifts up as you sit,
relieved and smiling, and says,
Oh yeah, those onion rings were good. Phew. Yeah.
Charles Bukowski said there's
nothing quite like a good beer shit.
Wrote about how the odor spreads
all around and stays for a good hour and a half.
He's right, of course, but a good onion ring shit tops it,
not so much for staying power,
which is about the same, but for its subtle,
sweet tang that differs ever-so-slightly
from that of the drank-25-beers-last-night
Bukowski good beer shit.
Both, though, serve as good reminders
that you're lucky to be alive.
Lucky, too, that everything turns to shit.

After Every Overdose

After every overdose someone has to clean up. Things just don't go back to normal, after all. Someone has to clean out the abandoned apartment so the rotting dreams don't stink up someone else's life. Someone has to put on rubber gloves and open the drawers, careful of used needles. Someone has to get mired in dirty clothes, unpaid bills, brimming trashcans, spoiled food and unflushed toilets. Someone has to pay the landlord and talk to the cops. Pretty it's not, and takes time. Hearts go ragged from feeling the pain. Someone, broom in hand, has to recall the way it was. Someone listens and nods. But already there are those who will find it dull, just the same old addict thing. Those who knew what was going on now make way for those who will never know. Or want to know. And in the room that has outgrown explanations, someone must be stretched out, gazing at the stars beyond the ceiling of it all.

At The End

At one point the whole entryway
was a loud, intoxicating mix of conversation,
cologne, perfume, reefer, and beer.
Suits, white shirts, and neckties
to beer shirts, cutoffs, and flip-flops.
Bankers, roofers, plumbers, teachers,
carpenters, secretaries, bikers, janitors, and nurses
(most all of them inked)
came teary-eyed or full of false bravado
to hug and hear in his eulogy about how
Duke never met a stranger
and once got Tiffany out of jail
so she could be with her kids on Christmas.
At the end, I helped carry flowers and plants
to his daughter's truck, roll his casket
back behind the partition,
and gather up the visitor sign-in book.
Some of the signatures were cursive, some printed.
Several signed one name only: Braxton, Ike, Chapi,
Jeremiah, Mad Dog, Digger. One just a squiggly line
that drifted lazily over half the page
before angling sharply to the bottom corner
like a dove shot out of the blue Kansas sky.

Grief

- for Karen

She brought me his CDs
of Burroughs, Malcolm X, and Kerouac.
I watched her trudging up the walk,
in a gifted veil she could not give back.

I Like Your Hat

I've been thinking about the way, when you walk down a crowded grocery aisle, you see people not wearing masks even though we're in the midst of a pandemic.

And how a wearer with his nose exposed will give you a dirty look when you suggest they cover it. The same kind of person who, when you drop your groceries, will just watch you pick them up.

We all have this person inside us. The one who wants to hang out with his friends at the bar and be handed a beer ice cold, and not have to say thank you to the server. The one who doesn't let you get into the flow of traffic on the on ramp.

Most of the time, though, we are able to hold back, and turn these moments into little kindnesses like,

Sorry.

Here, let me help.

Thank you.

and

I like your hat.

Give Me Some Guidance

Give me some guidance on health today,
I want to get really pissed off.
I want to rage and pout,
and I want you to love me
all the more for it.

Do you hear what I'm saying?
Speak to me about the benefits
of arugula, filtered water, and yogurt.
About giving up coffee, red meat,
carbohydrates, and sugar.

Tell me again that shit
about portion control.
I'm going to ask you over for
a large plate of pasta and a steak
with lots of garlic bread and
chocolate cake for dessert.
All you can eat.

Oh, I'm going to be a son of a bitch.
Tell me how aerobic exercise
is good for my arthritis,
and increases my energy.
How yoga feeds both body and soul.
How resistance exercise is good for my heart.

I'm going to lie down and take a nap
right here on the kitchen floor.

Catalpa Blossoms

Old man
in plaid cap
eases walker
down
sidewalk
littered
with
catalpa blossoms
gripping
Western Flyer
handlebars
his face
luminous
as he
pedals
hard
for
home.

When This Happens

My mother has a tendency
to be displeased that
waits patiently inside her
for me to drop my guard.
So just when I'm
expecting a simple
Thank you,
or nod of approval,
she bursts forth with
You've never helped me
that fuckin' much anyway.

Rather than bite the hook,
I become Inspector Clouseau
to her Cato and
we do verbal jujitsu.
I lean away
from her shame
with a little dance,
rather than step in
to take it full force.

Psychotherapy
has helped
to see it as
still another way
to find myself
in our interwoven
timelines of grief.

Also, not let the pain she's
inflicted over the years
prevent me from
treasuring
the times we've shared
something gentle.

Today she told me,
*Get out of my house
and never come back!*
I just smiled, said,
Okay, see you tomorrow.

Just Happy It Starts

Rebecca, one of my mother's new caregivers, came up from Louisiana with her two kids to live with her mother six months ago. Drives a 2004 Crown Vic, the faint watermark of the Louisiana Highway Patrol emblem on the door. I noticed the driver's side window was down one cold December morning just before Christmas as I walked to the house. When I asked about it she said, in a slow Slidell drawl, that she was waitin' on her paycheck to buy a part so she could fix it herself. Said her daddy was a mechanic. Fixed the rear end differential on it herself — with just a little help from a friend to drill out a sheared bolt. Don't you get cold? I asked. *Naw, I gotta old quilt to wrap around me when I drive. I'm just happy it starts.*

Out There On The Rim

In a used Crown Vic from the State Patrol
From Louisiana she did roll
Faint tattoo on her driver's side
Assorted dents underneath her hide
Had no reason, had no rhyme
Just desire and hills to climb
Had a big V8 and her foot was in it
No stop signs, no speed limit

> *And she don't care that she's walkin'*
> *Out there on a ledge*
> *Sayin' what's the use of livin'*
> *If you never find an edge*
> *She's hopin' that she can find it*
> *Somewhere on the rim*
> *Down the highway past the places*
> *She's already been been been*

Left the couch and all the dishes
Didn't stop to share good wishes
Or say goodbye to the guys that wooed her
They never did mean that much to her
With a couple kids and a Slidell drawl
She crossed the line into Arkansas
To stay with Momma in a bungalow
Blue jeans tighter than they were before

Say goodbye to Billy for her
He's the only one who never bored her
Playin' his beat up guitar
And singin' at the corner bar
Tell him to keep on playin' his songs
That they did a lot to right all her wrongs
Just keep that old Martin singin'
No matter what the blue days bring in

> *And she don't care that she's walkin'*
> *Out there on a ledge*
> *Sayin' what's the use of livin'*
> *If you never find an edge*
> *Hopin' that she can find it*
> *Somewhere on the rim*
> *Down the highway past the places*
> *She's already been been been*

No time to figure all the angles
Or get the whole damn mess untangled
No time to wait for judgment day
Just get out on that long highway
No time to fix what's already fractured
Or wait around to get raptured
Just ditch the Xanax and the Jack
And find out where she got off track

She Likes Me More Than Ever

Dementia has made Mother sweet
these last few months in contrast to
the ninety plus years of growling
and shaming her way through
raising seven kids while married
to a railroader on the road half the time.

Oh it's such a shame, my cousin told me sadly,
to see Aunt Helen's mind gone soft,
so simple and passive.

It is what it is, I responded.
Most days she doesn't recognize me
… but she likes me more than ever.

Sunday Morning Service Call

Just as Garrison Keillor started to recite "Old Blue" by William Stafford, I got a call from Mr. D that his car wouldn't start and he needed to get to church, so I loaded up the Labradorian for an Arlo and Noll Road Service call. D's car was up in his driveway just off the curb, so I pulled out the extra long jumpers liberated from my parents' Merc and stretched them across the yard telling D, "You know, I asked myself when I got these whatever was I gonna need a 20-foot set of jumper cables for and you finally answered the question." Then jumped in the Pathfinder and revved until he showed a thumbs up out his window. I unhooked, Arlo "Ruffed!" and I drove home to finish listening to Stafford's poem that begins: *Some day I'll crank up that Corvette, let it mumble those marvelous oil-swimming gears and speak its authority. I'll rock its big wheels till they roll free onto the drive.* Poem over, I thought about how much I miss the shift from first to second, clutch in, arm moving involuntarily up the three-on-the-tree post, followed by the smooth jerk to speed as I released the clutch. And going on from second to third, gas pedal trembling, clutch in, right arm levering instinctively down — the tug a little sweeter — as I accelerated toward the high-tingle of the quarter mile strip on the two-lane blacktop south of town.

Joining Mother In Her Dreams

I visit my mother
a couple of times a week
at the local nursing home
on the southeast edge
of reality.

Talking to her is like
trying to stay tuned
to a distant AM station
on an old transistor radio.

Yesterday she said
of her long dead sister-in-law,
That damn Georgie
keeps coming in here.
She won't leave me alone!

I said, *Okay, Mom,*
I'll have a talk with her.
Then she asked,
Where are your brothers and sisters?
And I said,
They'll be along in a while.
And she declared,
They damn well better be!

Some days when I go out
she's fast asleep,
a half smile on her face.

I quietly pull a chair
over next to her bed
close my eyes,
and join her
in her dreams.

Journey Of Desire

You were destined from your mother's womb
To arise and walk out of the tomb
With a smile so sweet and eyes aglow with fire
Some call you the Savior
I say you're the journey of desire

I wake in the morning to the church bell's ring
Realizing I still don't know a thing
And that there are no answers in the hymns of the choir
So I turn inward to the silence
And the journey of desire

I've found certain truths in a guru's walk
In poems and some of my pastor's talks
Truth is truth, no matter its attire
But it's the illusion in it all
That keeps me on the journey of desire

I may not call you up enough
Or turn to you when times get rough
But I wove you through my heart with lovely wire
That way I'm always bound to you
And the journey of desire

covid

coronavirus
social contagion of fear
time to sit, listen

toilet paper rolls
the currency of worry
in select-a-size

as roman hellos
elbow into our new world
six-foot masked man waits

tv teaching us
world geography of loss
tally of denial

cardinal singing
sweetly on the outstretched wing
of double parked plane

daffodil joy left
in pickle jar on back step
brings smile and deep sigh

my zen friend, ruben
ringing transformation bells
whom will they wake up?

Playing The Lottery

While waiting in line to buy a lottery ticket
at the local convenience store,
the man behind me leaned in and said,
What are you wearing that mask for?
Don't you realize that everyone has a chosen time
and God will decide when to take you?
I told him he could be right,
and that I would be happy to discuss it further
if he would please stand back six feet.
He sighed, shook his head and said,
Well … Jesus loves you.
Yeah, I know, I said. *Jesus loves everybody.*

Driving With Jesus

And if any man hear my words, and believe not
I judge him not: for I came not to judge the world,
but to save the world — John 12:47

Now the Bible is a darn good book
And a big one, sure it's true.
If you search it long enough
There's something there for you.
I looked myself at what Christ said
And after I was done,
I couldn't help but to conclude
That he loves everyone.

But love, you see, is dangerous
To start spreadin' around,
Wasn't that what Pilate feared
All the love He did expound?
It changes things to stop the hate
And power games, you see.
'Cause when you turn your heart to love,
Everyone is free.

But hate is truly easier.
Plus it protects the status quo.
If a person gives hate up,
Then he has to grow.
And if he starts to grow, could be
He'd start to understand.

Next he'd lose his ability
To shame and reprimand.

I know this would be losin'
Some things he holds so dear.
Not to mention the possibility
He'd have to face his fear.
And if he'd face his fear he'd need
People of all hues,
Blacks and reds and yellows,
Browns … and white ones, too.

Then there's straights and gays and lesbians,
The ones he's learned to rap,
The young, the old, the middle-aged
And those with handicaps.
Catholics, Jews and Muslims,
Buddhists and Baha'is.
Heck, before you know it,
He could be actin' just like Christ.

You know some people wonder
If He's comin' back someday.
I think he's already here
He drives a beat up Chevrolet.
On some days he's a black man.
On others he is white.
He's all colors of the rainbow
Included in pure light.

And does he shout, scold, and condemn
Or judge you from afar?
No, he just stops and says, "How about a lift?"
And you drive on in his car.

Mother's Day

- for Linda

Today,
take a break
from the jigsaw puzzle
of motherhood,
the clean house,
the made bed,
the well-cooked meal
    —the longing
for your children
to improve.

Instead,
let the whole thing
fall to pieces.

Go outside and look curiously
at the petunias,
cock your head at the geraniums,
place your feet anywhere
they've never been.

Lift your face to the sun
the way a sunflower
turns towards the eternal source,
speaking a language
no one else can understand.

On The 4th Of July

I won the 5K, and in record time. Not really. I made a hole in one on the par 3 final hole in the firecracker golf tournament. I wish. Some people gasped as I reached out of the window, while driving the street just outside the left field wall of JayCee ballpark, and caught a long homer bare-handed, after which my Lab, who was trying for it as well, snatched it out of my hand from the backseat window. Nope. At nightfall, I joined the musicians rocking from the band shell and launched into a Jimi Hendrix rendition of the *Star Spangled Banner* just as the fireworks display began over the park. Just kidding. But, I did visit Mom in the nursing home, share some smiles with the nurses and aides, assure Mr. Johnson I'd phone his accountant, and accept, from Fern, the *Reader's Digest* she thrust toward me from her wheelchair, saying, *Here, you need to read this!*

Peachy

was so
fat for
so long
always begging
demanding
cat treats
looking like
she was
inflated as
she took
her half
out of
the middle
when we
passed in
the hallway
to Mother's
bedroom
so when
I cradled
her bony
body at
the vet
as she
died her
frail
meow
caught
in
my
throat.

Railroad Dream

My long dead father calls me every night
from the tracks east of town,
his voice a diesel's low-pitched bass
coming in from the north
faint as cat feet at first,
then resonating like the behemoth
he will always be
until I can hardly bear it,
my heart rattling like glass
in the window between us.
I'm sure he's trying to say something,
send me a message.
But before I can understand it
he's gone south,
his deep voice fading
into a railroad dream.

Why I Love Being Married To A Teacher
- for Linda

Because she can still cause a reaction in me,
a flutter followed by a deep call
to the edge of awkward truth,
when she talks about her pupils.

Because she lugs home her computer
to do lesson plans and
shows me pictures
of field trips and mathletes.

Because once, years ago on a Saturday,
she was just standing silent
in the living room and I asked,
Honey, what's wrong?
and she said,
Oh … I was just thinking
about one of my students.

Yes, briefly

Did hitting him help?
Did getting a loan help?
Did a new job help?
Did new clothes help?
Did taking medication help?
Did prayer help?
Did a promotion help?
Did going to jail help?
Did drinking whiskey help?
Did leaving help?
Did cosmetic surgery help?
Did moving to a different town help?
Did divorce help?
Did staying put help?
Did losing weight help?
Did therapy help?
Did keeping it out of the newspaper help?
Did having sex help?
Did a new cell phone help?
Did new glasses help?
Did reading books help?
Did going to church help?
Did getting re-married help?
Did smoking a cigarette help?
Did a restraining order help?
Did avoiding it help?
Did buying a gun help?

Did keeping it secret help?

Did spiritual guidance help?

Did getting lost help?

Did starting a war help?

Did buying a high definition TV help?

Did meditation help?

Did telling everyone help?

Did taking a long drive help?

Did poetry help?

Groovy

At the *Paradise Resale Shop*
a man sorts
through used paperbacks,
the tattoo on his forearm,
once a vow of
undying love,
now a reddish-blue
wound.

In the next booth
a woman flipping
through LPs,
comes across
Carole King's *Tapestry,*
tears up, and
begins to sing softly,
*I feel the earth move
under my feet...*

Song over,
the man leans
around the corner,
asks if she would join
him at Harry's Café'
for coffee.

Groovy, she says.

Question
– for Chicken Annie's

Whatever happened to the girls with armloads
of plates piled high with fried chicken,

the glasses of ice tea, water, 7-Up and Pepsi
sweating on little red trays, and what

became of the aluminum carts piled high
with dirty plastic dishes, the packed

silverware holders beside the freshly
cleaned and wiped Formica tables,

the Kotzman brothers scraping and
washing dish after dish, glass

after glass beneath the dim neon
way, way in the back, just off

the cutting and breading room
the summer I turned sixteen

and went to work night after night
cleaning tables at Chicken Annie's

in an old converted miner's house
just west of the Missouri line,

and where is the Italian farm girl
who rode with me in a '55 Chevy

after work and refused my kiss
at the back door when I dropped her off

at her grandparents' white bungalow
just south of the high school football field?

I Drift Across The Hardwood After Hearing About Jon Sherman's Death

At midnight the band quits playing and I drift
across the hardwood toward the door.

A woman in one of the booths tucked beneath
the balcony calls out, *Play one more for me.*
Just one more. Please.

Hearing Jon's tickled laugh, I turn toward the stage
to see him sitting back down at his drums,
nothing under his skin but light.

I Hear A Train A Comin'

Dad had to give up golf because of a bad back,
tremors and balance problems,
eventually ending up in a wheelchair.
After that came dementia and Sunset Manor nursing home.
Our time together from then on
was mostly trips to the doctor
or Sunday Mass at Sacred Heart.
As we rode, pieces of memory came in tatters,
like shreds of an old cardboard box
full of greeting cards, photographs, and song lyrics
left too long in a damp corner of the basement.

One day I showed up to take him to the cardiologist
and he didn't want to go. So, as I pushed his wheelchair
down the shadowed hall of the nursing home,
I had to stay to the center, else the nurse and I
would have to stop and peel his fingers free
of the handrail that ran along both sides of the corridor.
After I'd finally wrangled him into the passenger seat
of my old Explorer, fastened his seatbelt, stowed the
    wheelchair,
and buckled myself in, I started the car and said, *Okay,*
    here we go.
He gave me a thin smile and a strange steady look,
leaned over and spat on my cassette tapes in the center holder.
Okay, he nodded. *I'm ready.*

The day he died, the nurse called at 5 a.m.
I cried softly as I got dressed and headed for the hospital.
As I approached the Rouse Street rail crossing,
I heard the two longs, a short, and a long
of a diesel horn that said a KCS freight was approaching.
Rather than hurry through, I slowed
to watch the crossbar drop and the lights begin to flash.
Opened all my windows to hear the clanging bells
and low-frequency, diesel OOMMM of the locomotive
as it rolled slowly past, pulling a mile-long rock-a-bye
of rumbling, clanking, squealing cars.

I just turned 70. I put the TV volume up a little louder,
sometimes switching on the closed captioning
when I have trouble understanding.
And playing golf last week I began to quiver
ever so slightly while standing over a long iron.

I'm starting to grasp it. Deterioration and death are my future.
I'm on a freight train sticking my head out
of the conductor's side of the locomotive to see
where I'm going and how long it will be before I get there.
Dad is in the engineer's seat humming an old tune,
a half smile on his face, easing the throttle forward.

Postmortem

So when I die please don't go on
about how I was good to my father
or mother or brother or children.
Or loved by a lot of people.
Just say that I got captured early
by words and the sound of the human voice.
That I leaned on them my whole life
and, for the most part,
they never let me down.

You might mention
that, together, my wife and I
learned a lot about love.
How it ebbs and flows.
How laughter buoys it up
when it starts to drown
in the mundanity of it all.

Also that I loved people.
Loved them for their misjudgments
and frailties and failures
as much as for any of their achievements.

Plant my ashes in the earth
next to some others in the cemetery
who, like me, could never quite get it right.

Then sing a song
and recite a short poem.

This one, maybe.

Founding member of White Buffalo and award-winning columnist for *The Morning Sun*, **J.T. Knoll** is the author of *Paperboy, True Stories, Entry / Exit Point, Chorus Line, Where the Pavement Ends,* and *Fetch Crazy.* The collection *Ghost Sign,* co-authored with Al Ortolani, Adam Jameson, and Melissa Fite Johnson was selected as a Kansas Notable Book for 2017. He lives with his wife, Linda, and Arlo the Labradorian on Euclid's curve in Pittsburg, Kansas, where he is a professor emeritus at Pittsburg State University and operates Knoll Training and Consulting.